# Beneath One Layer:
## A Poetry Collection

# Beneath One Layer
## A Poetry Collection

### Aimee Ebron

**Virginia**

**2025**

Beneath One Layer: A Poetry Collection

Copyright © 2025 by Aimee Ebron.
All rights reserved. No part of this publication may be reproduced, distributed, or transmitted in any form or by any means, including photocopying, recording, or other electronic or mechanical methods without prior written permission of the publisher, except in the case of brief quotations embodied in critical reviews, certain other noncommercial uses permitted by copyright law.

This book is a work of creative expression. Any similarities to actual persons, living or dead, are purely coincidental unless otherwise acknowledged by the author.is book is a work of creative expression. Any similarities to persons living or unless otherwise notified by the author

Published by Aimee Ebron
First Edition
Printed in the United States of America

ISBN: 979-8-218-71658-5
Library of Congress Control Number: 2025913902

Aimee Ebron

# Acknowledgments

For everyone who opened their hearts to me and for those who hold a place for me in the space of their prayers, you keep me alive, and I am eternally grateful.

# Table of Contents

Introduction .................................................. 1-2

## Poetry Collection

Sit with It ........................................................ 3
Quiet Moments, Big Ideas ........................... 4
In Between ..................................................... 5
Nomadic Spirit ............................................... 6
Cycle of Normalcy ......................................... 7
The Wayward Child ....................................... 8
The Weight of Ink ......................................... 9
Walking Alone ............................................. 10
Comfort of Discomfort ............................... 11
Power of Reflection .................................... 12
Embracing the Shadows ............................. 13
Resilience Amidst Ashes ............................ 14
The Strength of Simplicity ......................... 15
For the Passionate Creators ...................... 16
Stepping Into the Unknown ...................... 17
Dearly Beloved ............................................ 18
In Silence ..................................................... 19
Far Away ...................................................... 20
Disloyalty ..................................................... 21
A Lifeline of Love ........................................ 22
Tears in Distant Lands ............................... 23
Unseen Struggles ........................................ 24
Genocidal Seeds .......................................... 25
The Burden of Performance ...................... 26
Wake Up ....................................................... 27
Conditional Grace ....................................... 28
Reclaim Your Power ................................... 29
The Game We Play ...................................... 30
I Choose Violence ....................................... 31
Unseen Woman............................................ 32
Breaking the Silence ................................... 33
Introvert's Manifesto .................................. 34
Her Sacrifice................................................. 35

Nature's Symphony .................................................. 36
The Essence of a Soft Life ...................................... 37
  Truth or Delusion? ............................................... 38
  Unsolicited Realities ............................................ 39
  Veils of Deceit ...................................................... 40
  Unspoken Truths ................................................. 41
  Entitlement ........................................................... 42
  No Blessings Here ................................................ 43
  Harvest of Consequences ................................... 44
  Judgment's Flame ................................................ 45
  Duality of Spirit ................................................... 46
  Chained to Distance ........................................... 47
Empowerment In Solitude ..................................... 48
  Another Life.......................................................... 49
  The Fabric of Light .............................................. 50
  And Why Not You? ............................................. 51
  Embrace the Darkness ....................................... 52
  The Absurdity Within ......................................... 53
  Navigating the Terrain ....................................... 54
  Claiming My Femininity .................................... 55
  Boiling Point ......................................................... 56
You Should Know Her ........................................... 57
  Can I Trust You? .................................................. 58
  Remember When? ............................................... 59
  Dismissive Avoidance ......................................... 60
  Living Off .............................................................. 61
  An Empath's Storm ............................................. 62
Sparing You or Loving Me ..................................... 63
  One More High .................................................... 64
  Stumbling Block .................................................. 65
The Labor of Confidence ....................................... 66
  Self-Affirming ....................................................... 67
  Abiding Lies ......................................................... 68
  Power in Awkwardness ...................................... 69
  Open Intimacy ..................................................... 70
Holding Space for the Mundane ......................... 71

Traitor ............................................................. 72-73
To My Tribe, With Love ....................................... 74
  Seeking Wholeness ............................................. 75
  Queendom ........................................................ 76
  Leave Me .......................................................... 77
  Real Love .......................................................... 78
For the Love of the Diaspora ................................. 79
The Illusion of Stability ........................................ 80
Unforgiving Shadows ........................................... 81

# Introduction

I've never considered my external life particularly interesting. My upbringing was typical of my time. Our family adhered to traditional values: we attended church, shared family dinners with both immediate and extended relatives, and spent more time playing outside than watching television. My dad worked for the city while my mom stayed home. Responsibility was paramount; consistency and a strong work ethic were expected. I learned early on that hard work was essential for sustaining myself in adulthood. In a way, my future felt predetermined: finish high school, get a job, marry, buy a home, have children, and work until retirement. Yet, despite this mapped-out life, I longed for something different. College wasn't an expectation in my family, but I eventually attended, albeit much later than most. To me, college was the only alternative path in sight that might offer divergency from the life I had known.

In contrast, my internal life was complex. Even as a child, I was acutely observant, noticing things that would take years to process—issues most children overlook. I grappled with thoughts I struggled to articulate, spending countless hours mulling them over. This constant contemplation made me willful, leading me to clash with societal norms. By the age of nine, I had encountered racism, sexism, and classism, though I lacked the vocabulary to define them. Instinctively, I recognized the need for self-protection and preservation, understanding that the world favored boys over girls and men over women. I began to see my parents as individuals—a man and a woman—rather than simply as "Mom" and "Dad." Around this time, I sensed a brewing conflict with God, accumulating a lifetime of questions but lacking sufficient answers.

This internal struggle has kept me in a constant state of overthinking. My fascination with writing emerged from this relentless pondering, cultivating a deep introspection within me. The thoughts I generated were so personal that I never intended

to share them. Much of what I wrote early on lacked the life experience and insight to convey my feelings accurately. Throughout my adult life, I have worked to recalibrate what I thought I knew from the lessons learned on my journey.
*Beneath One Layer* is a collection of poetry that captures glimpses of my conclusions on various issues. It reflects my perspective on the world, human experience, and my place within it.

## Sit With It

We all must reckon with life in the middle,
For it is the meat and sweet of the journey
The space between joy and pain,
The terrain between fear and courage,
The valley between failure and success.
Going through it speaks to survival;
Experiencing it speaks to growth.
Spiritual consciousness is understanding the difference;
If we are lucky, we discern when to pivot.

In reckoning with life in the middle,
We learn to find balance:
The space between flying and landing,
The terrain between solitude and loneliness,
The valley between taking and giving.
Self-accountability is self-love.
Knowing it happened for you is emotional intelligence.
Both cultivate reverence for life;
If we are blessed, we experience divinity.

## Quiet Moments, Big Ideas

Quiet little moments filled with grandiose ideas
lead to flashes of life that words cannot describe.
Instances that are seen, forgotten, and recalled again.

An understanding of the unfamiliar,
even while lacking a point of origin.
Resilience without a point of reference.

And thus, a wayward child is born
a human ark of the family covenant.
Willful watcher over the fabric of the village.
A witness to their existence,
more than a participant in their convictions.

## In Between

The truth is, I've always felt out of place
Like I'm lagging or oddly in between,
Never quite ending where I intended.
It's like moving without purpose.

I attempt to move instinctually,
But I never feel connected to where it takes me.
That's okay, I fare well enough.
Whether I understand it or not, I accept it.
This feels spiritual.
Does it all mean something?
Maybe it doesn't mean anything at all.
I could ponder this all day,
And I probably will.
The mind lingers, even when the body wanders.

This is where wisdom would tell me to surrender,
Yet I'm never sure how to do that.
What does surrendering look like?
I should get comfortable with not having all the answers,
But it feels like I never have any answers,
and that's a different thing.

It's been said that I have an old soul,
But I guess I've aged into it.
I am too old to be a child,
But too clueless to be an adult.
It's like being in a space filled with wisdom,
Yet not understanding how I got there,
while still knowing, I am somewhere.

# Nomadic Spirit

People wonder about my tendency to leave home,
but my home is everywhere and nowhere.
I don't belong to one place or another;
I belong wherever I go.
I stay for a time,
but that time has passed,
now I need to be free.
I must leave to find myself within.
Before, I didn't understand this nomadic spirit,
as I do now;
It didn't have a place of its own,
it just was.

## Cycle of Normalcy

Naturally, if you can call it that,
We do what needs to be done to have a normal life.
Whatever is meant by a normal life.
Whatever is acceptable as normal.
We put ourselves aside for the predictable,
assuming we desire the predictable.
Yet, here we are, much later,
realizing our predicament.
None of us wanted this.
Yet, someone created the to-do list,
And we did it; we keep doing it
Over and over.

## The Wayward Child

Whatever happened to the wayward child?
How did she fare as she aged?
Did she fall in love and have her heart broken?
Did she leave a trail of broken hearts?
Perhaps she finally fell apart,
pieces of her scattered about.
Did she learn any lessons from what caused her to shatter?
Is she on her own now, still bearing the weight of others?
Has she fallen out of the grace of her father and mother,
Or is she a crutch for her sisters and brothers?
And what of her friends
did she make any?
Are there people who carry her in the space of their prayers?
Did she vanish into addictive squalor and promiscuity,
or has she turned pain into passion,
becoming a well of possibility?
I'd like to know where the wayward child stands,
for the fate of her fortune was left in her hands.

## The Weight of Ink

Writing these words in hopes of shaking loose
what's stuck on the inside.
Maybe, just maybe, I can feel again,
or perhaps feel something real for the first time.
Pen to page is like knife to skin;
Flowing emotion is the bleed-out.
The blood stains the page,
Revealing that my generational inheritance is intrinsic pain

## Walking Alone

Loneliness covers me today.
Not because people aren't around,
or because their intentions aren't good,
they simply do not walk in my shoes.
Shoes that these tired feet have worn to tatters.

I've walked a million miles on a road
where no one is just ahead to guide me,
or beside me to keep watch.
There is no one behind
to encourage me to keep going.
It's a deserted road where I encounter faces,
familiar yet strange.
Faces that have never heard of where I'm going
faces heading in a different direction.
Sure, many have felt alone like this,
but not in *this* way.
This is my "sometimes you have to walk alone" moment.

## Comfort of Discomfort

Seldomly, do I find comfort in the familiar voices
and the arms of those who love me.
Perhaps it's because they know too much.
They've seen me like a wilting plant:
Underwatered, underfed, and overexposed.
It isn't something you can unsee,
even if one bounces back
and begins to flourish.
I'd rather be lost among the faces of strangers,
Who can only settle that I look or seem familiar.
They'd be too polite to intrude past a gentle "hello."

I'd rather sit quietly, composing my life's song
From the varying instruments of questions that occupy my mind.
The distance between me and the fulfillment of that wonder,
is my fear of floating away
never being able to land.

What if others, who aren't mine, see me?
What if they can see that I was once a wilted plant?
It feels safer to stick closely to the familiar voices
and the arms of those who love me.
It's the place where I know the discomfort,
And I've learned to manage it well.
The only requirement is the assimilation to responsibility,
Which I have mastered in my mostly utilitarian life.

## Power of Reflection

There is a song that makes me pause and ponder.
Some would call it sad or somber,
But I thrive in the space of introspection.
The song isn't somber or sad; it is mere recollection

## Embracing the Shadows

Everyone wants to bask in light,
But I gravitate toward the darkness.
The light inside me is all I need.
Dark rooms with blackout curtains,
candles lit for ambiance.
Not just physical darkness,
I hide my mind in shadowed spaces
And observe my own heart of darkness.
I allow myself the chance to play both ends:
Darkness and light, good and evil.

## Resilience Amidst Ashes

Many hopes burned to ashes,
Dreams faded into nightmares.
Lights dimmed by circumstance,
Expectations deferred happiness
And still, we've made progress.

## The Strength of Simplicity

There is power in the simple things:
Modesty in a world where relevance
requires a thinner moral code.
Saying how you feel –
being vulnerable,
in a world that has grown cold.

Sharing knowledge and information
to help others grow,
Sowing seeds from the harvest
you've reaped one hundredfold.
There is power in silence:
Holding your tongue when you're triggered,
Practicing restraint when you've had enough.
Introspection and self-correction
when you've done too much,
Taking a break from the friction
With those you love,
Pressing forward in wisdom
Without giving up.

## For the Passionate Creators

I create for those who do it because they love it.
They make the music they want to dance to,
Painting life with their own colors.
Their vibe resonates beyond the status quo.
Even if they are the only ones, they do it anyway
With the same passion, the same perfectionism,
And the same focus.
They don't need to be seen, because they are felt.
Their impact on those fortunate enough to experience them
is unequivocal.

## Stepping Into the Unknown

You'll find me stepping off the ledge,
Free falling,
Head over heels for joy, for peace, for freedom.
You'll find me out of sight,
Away from the limelight and nightlife,
Off camera, behind the scenes, clinging to myself.
You won't know my face,
But you'll know my work.
You'll recognize my vibe;
My energy will feel welcoming and familiar.
You'll know my creativity; it will be breathtaking,
A far-reaching mystery.

## Dearly Beloved

Dearly beloved,
We are gathered in mutual trauma.
Here we unlearn, relearn, expose, and impose.
We love hard and easily offend,
And normalize everything.
We get unhinged, we cancel and are canceled.
Our natural state is overstated,
And we engage in ignorant debates.
We gather in abundance of spirit.
We are creative, innovative, combative, and empathic.
We are spiritually inclined yet blindly delusional,
Shrugging while being fascinated by the eccentric and unusual.
As usual, we are both inclusive and exclusive,
Cliquish and childish,
And let's not forget, all who gather are stylish.
This gathering is an epic story,
Part of our generational glory.
The horror of whoredom is boredom.
We are born in clicks and slides,
Scrolling as we die,
Screaming eye for an eye.
This is where our insides are worn outside,
while the outside is passing us by.

## In Silence

You don't value my voice,
if sweet words aren't tickling your ears.
You don't appreciate my song,
if I do not sing your praise.
You turn a deaf ear to my screams
if they hold you accountable.
Yet you question my silence.

You are offended
by my refusal to answer your call.
You don't want to hear me humming
because it isn't your favorite tune.
You don't listen to my concerns
because the solution wouldn't serve you.
You don't accept my truth
because it breaks down the walls of your wrongs.

Yet you chastise me for my silence,
when you think I should defend you.
And still, from your point of view,
my silence is violent.

# Far Away

I'm far away.
I'm so far away
Further than the depth of a volcanic floor,
Far from space beyond space.
I feel *that* far away,
Like no one can ever find me.
Maybe I'm far away
for a purpose that's not my own.
I feel like I'm far enough away.
Far like I'm supposed to be.
Don't you feel far away?
It can't only be me.
Tell me you feel far away too.

## Disloyalty

This sucks.
I pray for you,
Cry for you,
Hurt for you,
Love on you.
I fight with you,
I fight for you,
I laugh with you,
I nurture you.
I've accepted you,
I've forgiven you,
and I've shown up for you.
Time and again,
you broke me.
Cursed me,
Ignored me,
Abused me.
You used me,
You hurt me,
You disrespected me,
You laughed at me,
You lied to me,
And deserted me.

Your disloyalty hurts.

## A Lifeline of Love

When I observe your way,
what you say, what you do,
and how you move
I'm critical of you.
My criticism comes from a place of love,
adoration, conviction, and faith.
I believe in you and see you winning
Before you even show up for the race.
I wish you'd put down the baggage;
The anger isn't yours to carry.
Visionary, I know you glimpsed greatness—so did I.
I carry it, nurture it, and nest for it;
I am prepared for its birth.
Don't abandon it now.
I roll my eyes and grab my waist in a rage;
My passion and my being are deeply connected to you.
If you don't survive,
I fear it will be the death of me.
Remember that every time you decide.
Before you make your next move, remember me.
Think of yourself as my lifeline.
I was born to stand beside you,
To help you maneuver.

## Tears in Distant Lands

It took going to a distant land
for me to release real tears -
Silent tears,
overflowing tears.
Free as the wind,
in the company of strangers.
Away from my comfort zone,
off this land.
I cried real tears,
Silent tears,
overflowing tears.

## Unseen Struggles

If you didn't have a visual, could you see me?
Could you know the heaviness of sorrow I carry
If you couldn't see the tears forming in my eyes,
could you feel the ache of my soul?
If you didn't see me flinch at your gaze…
If you couldn't hear my voice,
could you hear my wailing?
Could you grasp the case I pleaded,
if I never uttered a word?
Is my spirit familiar to you?
Can you read my energy?

## Genocidal Seeds

You delusional fool,
what did you expect?
You planted, watered, fertilized,
and pruned a seed of hate.
Why would you expect a harvest of love?
How could you believe
you be met with adoration?

We all saw and we remember
We all felt it and wear scars.
No one forgives you.

May God's wrath fall heavy on your head.
May darkness fall so heavy on you
that you assume you've lost your sight.
You are the very hate you suffered –
are you proud of that?
When it's all said and done,
what have you gained?
Those who have shown themselves as comrades today
will be tomorrow's enemies.
This is my decree.

## The Burden of Performance

What they see is that you've mastered your craft.
They have no clue about the uptick of anxiety,
The aftermath of you reenacting…
The violence against Black bodies.

High-pressure to press into your wounds,
Swinging hard to protect others
while you bleed out on screen -
where you can't scream.
You can't cry, or fight, or break anything.
Game face on game day as you replay the same pain.
Yours and mine and theirs,
you are ours.

In that hour, you are the community,
And it isn't lost on me
That even though you can't breathe,
You smile and share niceties
just to eat.

## Wake Up

Girl, he doesn't love you,
And it's not that he doesn't want to
he doesn't know how.
You can't teach him,
you don't know how either.
All that lying and manipulating,
Sexing to control,
All those gender roles,
Favor-for-favor bullshit you both engage in.
Just two fools pretending.
Grow up.
Learn love.
Learn you.
And then come back.
Without the drama,
Without the tears,
Without the lies,
Without the weird and stale energy.

## Conditional Grace

You're staring…waiting for my approval.
I withhold it, intentionally.
to hurt you.

In a split second,
I think of all the things that I've endured.
You're an incompetent partner.
I don't mind mistakes,
but all you've done is lie and deflect.
Your narcissism has been appalling.
I'm stalling…

A part of me hated you.
After all of the grief,
you've decided to grow.
And now you're looking for grace
I'm not sure I'm capable.
I said I would try
I won't.

You're waiting for a smile,
Something to validate this moment,
I'm disgusted & you don't even know it.
I loathe you
I was hoping that I'd leave before you changed
But I didn't.
Do I now owe you?

## Reclaim Your Power

They make you hate your strength,
hoping that you'll abandon it.
They can't stand you with it.
It's being used against you instead of for you.
Change the game with it.
Break their plans with it.

## The Game We Play

The words falling from your lips are poetic
Lyrical lies flying by my ears.
You want me to be convinced,
And for a second, I play your game.
And though it sounds deranged,
Just for you, I do petty too.
I let you believe that I believe;
I let you think I've been deceived.
And just before you reap your reward,
I pounce on your masculinity.

I call you on every shortcoming,
I hit below the belt and turn the table.
And still, I will be the victim.
The vindictive outcome will work for me;
This is the hell of your making.

# I Choose Violence

I believe in God
but, I am human.
I have an imperfect faith,
and the power of free will,
I choose violence.

Where it concerns our enemies,
let the ground beneath their feet burn
Let them fall into the pits of hell
that is their portion.
It is a seed they planted

Serve them like the Amalekites
Deal with them ever so severely
Shackle them to the weight of their hearts.
Snatch away their sheets and badges
Let the world see them naked
For those who carry the spirit of Jezebel
Let their pain be relentless

Chain their hiding hands.
Stone them with the rocks they've stored.
Let a portion of our victory be their downfall.

If more of us must die,
let us take them with us.
My ancestors were forced to fight or fall
many fought and lost so that I might live.
For them, I will live, survive, and prosper.
And for the sake of those coming after me,
I choose violence.

## Unseen Woman

Rumor has it she is cursed,
Unwanted and not blessed.
Her accomplishments void of celebration
For what does it mean without a man?
What is the purpose with no children?
Without her input, her femininity has been defined,
And why should anyone ask her?
What does she know?
If she has never had children, nor been married,
What wisdom lies within her?
She stands accused, judged, sentenced,
an agent of her own oppression.
How dare she build without a man?
How dare her plans not preset for children?
A menace, a witch, an imposter
a bad influence, a useless part of society.
Why should society consider her?
Why should society hear her?
Why should society plan for her?
Why should society bless her name?
Why should her time be her own?
For what will she contribute with no man?
With no child to give her actions purpose,
who is she?

## Breaking the Silence

Grin and bear it.
No pain, no gain—right?
Take the high road.
Brush your shoulders off.
Leave it in the past.
That is the ask.
Your scars are beauty marks.
Get over it.
Fake it 'til you make it.
Pray through it.
Grow from it.
Forgiveness is a virtue
That is how they get you.
Before you know it, you are sucking down oppression,
Calling it life lessons,
Stinking up the place with a bad attitude.
And they wonder why you're drenched in depression,
Complaining and incubating hate.
Walking around in some type of mood.
You are filled with aggression,
Feeling less than,
Barely getting through.
This is what not speaking up gets you.
But forget all the antidotes
And quotes they say on cue!
Express yourself.
Say what you need to say.
Feel how you need to feel.
Hold them accountable
Out loud!

## Introvert's Manifesto

I am an introvert trying to survive in an extroverted world, so...
If I am forced to engage with a low social battery,
every word out of my mouth will be laced
with irritability, sarcasm, apathy.

Invite me, but I'm not coming.
If I show up, it'll be on time,
and I'll be the first to leave.
I won't be disappointed if you cancel plans.
I will most certainly zone out of the conversation.
I do not have a face of flint
annoyed, content, and daydreaming,
come with the same expression.

I'm not shy; I'm observant and introspective.
I'm confident and humble.
I'm quiet, not dumb.
If you want to spend time with me,
keep it simple, don't invite extra people.

## Her Sacrifice

The world is cursed.
Do you want to know how I know?
Because I am a Black woman.
You'll never know the pain of being unloved
by a world you birthed.
We've reincarnated for a thousand lifetimes
to prevent that hurt.

Our body is the earth, the water, the air, the fire.
Every abuse of the land is a scar on us.
Our DNA has lent itself to everybody,
and yet, you despise us.
Even when we knew trouble would ensue,
we traveled back to protect you.

We could have easily stayed away
while the ground sank into the sea,
while the ocean boiled over,
and fire burned everything.

We could have stepped aside
as the wind stirred up dangerous debris.
But you will never know that tragedy
we have always stood with you,
even when you've abandoned us.

## Nature's Symphony

I smell rain.
I see patterns mimicked in tree vines and leaves.
I can hear the wind blow.
I feel the sun's heat, even on cold days.
I can taste the atmosphere.

## The Essence of a Soft Life

Soft life for me is simply doing what needs to be done
at my own pace,
in my own time,
with my own wit,
with my own faith,
without chains,
without expectation,
without ego,
without questions,
without gripes,
without complaints,
without explanation.
I move forward in faith,
doing what needs to be done,
basking in the joy of knowing I chose this path.

## Truth or Delusion?

When you ask for my advice,
do you want me to tell you the truth,
or do you want me to camp with you
in your delusion?

## Unsolicited Realities

Allow me to gaslight you, if that's what this is.
If you don't want unsolicited advice,
stop using other people's ears as your garbage can.
If you think someone shouldn't give marriage advice,
stop babbling about your marriage to them.
If you think someone shouldn't give parenting advice,
stop trying to include them in your village.

Those withdrawals without deposits are expensive;
high cost, slow return with no interest.
You're upset about intellectual pragmatism,
but you continue to entertain chaos
in a way that's unhinged.

## Veils of Deceit

Loyalty to country requires a stance against terrorism,
both foreign and domestic.
Yet those who demand the oath,
clearly didn't understand the message.

You pit the "least among you" against one another
and convince some to take pride in your decisions.
The devil is in the details,
you sneaky parishioners and politicians.

You've hidden in plain sight.
I consider the coverings of those who hide in synagogues
to be the worst abiding lies and chaos.
They were the first to be adorned with pedigree
and a suit of privilege.

## Unspoken Truths

Are we supposed to pretend that none of it happened?
What are we to do with the pain,
the weight, and the disparity?
How can we maneuver around the cognitive dissonance
that reopens our wounds?

Is the ask forgiveness?
And if so, doesn't that require confession of sin?
Doesn't it require making amends?
It's violent to ignore what's still an
insurmountable, present indiscretion.

How do you make up for centuries of brutality and trauma?
How do we heal from any of it?
All of it built a society where
we are still not welcomed.

How do you retract the lies?
How do you retract the poison you soiled us with?
How do you diminish the capacity
and judge harshly the inability to function properly?
What is the expectation?

# Entitlement

I've been waiting for this day.
I knew it was coming the audacity of your expectations.
You withheld vital parts,
you stole crucial information,
you destroyed the possibility of an existence
without trauma and pain.
You watched me struggle and scramble.
I worked, I bled, I sweated, and I cried.
I studied, researched, stood tall, and made it.
I did it, afraid, and I did it alone.
I did it despite you, and despite everything,
and now I finally have the glow of victory.
Yet you feel entitled to stand with me.
What gives you the right?
How are you not sick with regret?
The world that is made for you stood by your side
while you harvested and swallowed energy,
like a supplement for your existence.
You did not bleed.
You did not sweat or cry.
You did not study,
or stand for anything.
Yet, you believe you deserve everything.
How are you not embarrassed?
Why aren't you ashamed?
You are guilty guilty of it all!
You are not so different from your ancestors;
you are not so free from the chains.
Your hand has never been on the plow,
nor your hand on the gavel,
but you have stood in the crowd bearing witness
as those who chained me took my power.

## No Blessings Here

Absolutely not! I am not a patriot.
This stolen land evolved,
using the energy it harvested,
on the souls it consumed.
An animalistic genocide
of bodies that were forcibly taken and rearranged.
Every system built since
has been governed by the deranged.
I dare not scream,
"God bless anything."

## Harvest of Consequences

I do not cast spells and curses even though
there is power in my tongue to do so.

There is no magic potion or wand needed
to watch you reap the harvest that you've sown.

You are the descendants of psychopaths,
sociopaths and lunatics.

You've made your way using smoke, mirrors,
bad doctrine and political rhetoric.

You hoard wealth and power like it can
or would provide you with protection.

But your mediocre thinking didn't count for
unnatural disasters and spiritual insurrection.

It's a shame you'll still fail at life
when you had the favor of a learning curve.

But it's not my bag to hold, so I'll grow old
watching you have the ending that you deserve.

## Judgment's Flame

When the world burns,
the fire will start in the church.
This will not be a Holy Spirit fire.
This will be a fire of judgment,
because you continue to preach lies.
You uphold hypocrisy, oppression, and manipulation.
You preach, "God will not be mocked,"
and then stare into the faces of His people,
leading them to slaughter.

## Duality of Spirit

My heart and mind are both clear;
my spirit is settled.
I no longer need to know all the moving parts
or the intricate details of what happened.
One truth remains: no matter the lessons learned
or the lies uncovered,
God is real.

I don't blame God or Satan;
I blame the tendency in human nature
to entertain good and evil as it suits us.
Diabolical evil can only be met
with radical love and radical goodness,
And yes, even righteous violence.

Yet we dance with fear and escapism
instead of facing it head-on.
We cling to doctrine and egotistical paradigms
rather than trusting in true freedom.
We make concessions for those
with pedigree and nice suits,
who commit the unthinkable out of greed,
while judging, convicting, and criminalizing
those who have been their victims.
We point fingers and assign blame
instead of self-assessing
and improving ourselves accordingly.
Somehow, we carry both the spirit of God
and the spirit of Satan,
when we should carry only one, exclusively.
Still, we call on God with evil in our hearts,
thinking nothing of our own hypocrisy.

## Chained to Distance

I knew someone like you once - cold and distant,
unable to let anyone get too close.
The irony is that people are drawn to your energy;
they want to know you, though they may not discern the truth.
You didn't stop them,
because a part of you craved connection too.

Unfortunately, you've never believed that warmth,
compassion, and empathy could be yours -
not while living in a constant state of brutal survival.
You've consistently stepped on toes,
acting vindictively toward those
whose actions you misunderstood.

Building and then burning the bridge
between you and the possibility of love.
It's a reckless existence,
having so many enemies trapped in the same cage as you.

Your freedom is tied to your ability
to let go of what no longer serves you,
yet you don't know who you are without the baggage and chains.
So, all you stand to gain in this life
is everything that drives you insane.

## Empowerment In Solitude

Sis, we need to talk

You know how some of the others
vote against their own best interests
to maintain privilege?
It works against them repeatedly,
but they keep doing it despite our warning?

We are doing the same...
when we keep yelling at our oppressors
to take us out of the chains.
I mean do we really want in
on these systems and spaces?

We should just bow out gracefully and disappear.
We should find a place where we would be forgotten
Left to grow in our power
Let the pick me, delusional, bitterly surviving,
woman-hating women have this hour.
Let them seek out the ones who continue to devour.

I'm not speaking against love and partnership.
I'm speaking against the violence of
depending on our attackers to defend us.

The price we've already paid with our labor and freedom
has never been enough - they want everything.
Even the spirit that keeps us as us.

I'm saying strengthen self, heal self, love self, redeem self,
and honor self, for thyself.

## Another Life

In another life, I loved you.
We held hands beneath the misty rain,
sharing dreams and offering unwavering support.
We laughed at those who couldn't understand us
enigmatic souls, split in two,
tethered together in a world that couldn't grasp our bond.
We thrived in that connection.
In another life, you loved me.
We wrote poetry in the quiet moments apart,
reciting verses in the park when we reunited.
Our words flowed effortlessly,
sentiments always understood.
We embraced through life's storms,
always emerging together,
and my God, how we cherished it.
In that other life, where love enveloped us,
we savored it all.
In this life, I don't know your name,
nor can I recall your face.
Yet my spirit aches,
haunted by the absence of my other half.
In this peculiar space,
I find myself alone.
Love feels unattainable,
its allure lost in the mundane.
Now I remain indoors as the rain falls softly,
writing poetry for an audience of none,
adrift in the winds of solitude,
unmoved by the storms that surround me.

## The Fabric of Light

I can share my secrets with you,
and I know you'd hold them deep within,
covering them with grace,
making it feel effortless for me to exist under your skin.
With you, I am safe—not just from words unspoken,
but from the very essence of who you are;
your nature bears good fruit,
and I find comfort in that truth.
There's a part of you that wishes to change,
to fit others' expectations,
not to forsake them, but to belong.
You're good that way,
though you might not even realize it.
That's the beauty of you.
You've wondered if you're good enough
to be counted among the righteous,
and you dare not imagine
being seen as one of the greats.
But you are.
You truly are.
Even if someone were to turn you inside out,
you wouldn't falter, you wouldn't fail.
You don't grasp how you weave into the fabric of the world,
how someone who seems to fade into cloudy days
can bring sunshine in the presence of the moon.
Yet, you do.
You illuminate the dark,
a quiet brilliance that transforms everything.

## And Why Not You?

And why shouldn't it be you?
Your scars matter,
each one is a testament to survival.
You've faced storms,
weathered disasters.
You emerged, though shattered,
still standing.
So why not now?
Why not embrace the strength
born from your trials,
the resilience woven into your being?
You are worthy of the light,
of the love that awaits,
a new chapter just beyond the horizon.
Let your journey unfold
you've earned it.
Step forward,
for it is your time.

## Embrace the Darkness

Work through all of it.
Cry every tear that's bound to surface.
Searching inward may bring suffocating pain,
but the healing that follows is worth the struggle.
I know what it's like to dwell in a dark place,
where every thought feels like an existential crisis,
the kind that drives you to your vices.
It all festers in the corners of your mind,
pulling the light from your spirit,
leaving you to wonder if it's better to silence it,
even if it risks your own light fading away.
But know this:
the darkness is a part of your journey,
not the end of it.
You have the strength to rise,
to let the tears cleanse your soul,
to find your way back to the light.
Embrace the work,
and let the healing begin.

## The Absurdity Within

I hide the absurd with a play on words,
my therapy when I feel unheard.
In moments of hurt,
from physical upset
to emotional neglect,
my mental defects
trigger spiritual resets.
Through laughter and lines,
I weave my release,
transforming my pain
into poetic peace.
In the dance of language,
I find my way back,
healing the wounds
that life tried to stack.

## Navigating the Terrain

There is no safe space for me
just places I inhabit,
places I must traverse,
and familiar haunts.
It's relatively simple:
if I am quiet and speak softly,
if I tiptoe and choose my words kindly,
I can navigate the landmines.

## Claiming My Femininity

You accused my femininity of being masculine,
because my strength, heart, courage, stamina, logic,
protectiveness, boldness, passion, and desire
didn't fit into your narrow box.
But my strength does not negate my pain.
My heart does not erase my needs.
My courage does not diminish my softness.
My stamina still craves rest.
My logic remains balanced by emotion.
My protectiveness seeks acceptance.
My boldness yearns for respect.
My passion desires support.
My sexual appetite is vibrant and expressive.
My femininity is fluid and full,
powerful, great, mighty, and unrelenting.
It is ever-present, boiling over,
covering everything in my path.
I am fully feminine, regardless of attire,
hair, curves, or the lack thereof.
There is no debt to pay for the agency over my femininity.
It belongs to me.
It is mine to define as an individual,
not a weapon for you to wield against me.

## Boiling Point

I've turned my head a thousand times,
Trying not to see lives being sifted.
I am not afraid;
I'm angry, and my blood boils.
My indignation rages.

## You Should Know Her

She stands reigning,
A regal beauty bound to the earth,
Magic stained by pain,
Yet her light remains magnificent.
Not one to shy away from the work
You should know her.
She is pregnant
with life, with vision, with hope,
Carrying the weight of strength.
Still, her will to build is unrelenting,
steadfast and immovable in belief
You should know her.
She is the embodiment,
A representation of God's power,
Moving in spirit and purpose,
Notwithstanding the forces against her,
A face of flint against danger
You should know her.

## Can I Trust You?

Can I trust you?
If I lay my burdens down,
If I set myself aside,
Do you promise to fight for me?
For my freedom?
For my sovereignty?
Can I trust you?
My woman ancestors
Laid down their burdens;
They set themselves aside,
Then were left to fight for themselves.
They were accused of divisiveness,
Verbally bashed and beaten.
And now... I'm not as keen to
Can I trust you?

## Remember When?

Remember when you wanted to die?
You screamed to the sky, "Take me."
You thought you couldn't make it, but you did.
Remember when you thought your current age was old?
The aches, pains, scars, and gray hairs
You didn't think you'd live to see it, but you did.
You're built for it, you know?
Survival, not just survival, but spirited thriving.
If you look closely, you see the light; you do.

## Dismissive Avoidance

I shrug and shake,
I pull and push away.
Don't lean on me;
Don't need me for a thing.
I twist and turn,
I avoid and evade.
Don't lean on me;
Don't need me for a thing.

## Living off Almost

Yeah, there's a roof over my head,
but it isn't mine.
I've always wanted to live in this area,
people call it a prime location,
but it isn't mine.

This is close, so close, to my dream location,
but this situation isn't it,
and this isn't the exact spot.

Oh, I'm grateful,
it could be another way.
Still, I'm resentful because,
it should be another way.

Who would have thought that in this space of life,
I'd be living off the grace of almost?
All I own is a room in a location
Close to, but not exactly where I wanted to be.
So close and still thousands of miles away.

## An Empath's Storm

I hate this feeling of fragility.
It's heavy, like a winter coat squeezed over too many layers.
It's kind of unnecessary, you know? Because of the layers.
But to anyone looking, it seems appropriate.

No one would ever question me wearing it in this season;
it seems right for the weather.
There's still cold and wet fog,
and I'm standing in the middle of it.
Oddly, I'm barely recognizable.

The emotional debris causes me to cover my face.
The weight of it, this fragility,
is a cross to bear, and it isn't always mine.
For it comes from the east and west winds,
from snowfalls and sandstorms,
from heat waves and blowing rains.
Oh, the woes of an empathic soul.

## Sparing You or Loving Me

Whenever I try to walk away,
I look at you and can't make myself leave,
Even though I'm torn between
Sparing you and loving me.

I still must think about it…
Imagine that.
After all the hurt you've caused,
I'm still considering risking myself,
Thinking about what I could have done
to make it better.
Your eyes show no remorse,
But I'm still standing here,
Debating whether I should
Spare you or love me.

Your arrogance is evident,
Your selfishness still intact,
Both willing me to go.
You know I'd be lonely,
The straw that won't allow me
To love me and leave you.

## One More High

When I'm high, it doesn't hurt as much.
I can't feel the burning stings or the brokenness.
The taste on my lips is bitter, but forgetting is addictive.
In the sweet spot, right before I lose my senses,
I remember that once it was good
To measure fairly, good was just better than this.
Another bump, and I'm done.
Is this the faint before the fall?

## Stumbling Block

When you live your life in response to
what others have done,
what others think, and what others do,
you often sacrifice important parts of your character to do so.

Your actions come across as inauthentic,
and you easily feel offended when people call bullshit.
You're not living your best life; you're not "doing you."
You are acting out in rebellion to someone else's truth.
That is torture for you and for those on the sidelines.

# The Labor of Confidence

The truth is that real confidence takes work.
Imagine looking out into the world
and every image that is thought to be unattractive,
unappealing, and useless
matches what you see in the mirror.

Not that you agree, but you realize
that a great majority believe that about you.
You're taught to be kind, polite, and respectful,
but never encounter that from others.
Imagine devaluation of your gifts and talents
because you aren't the *right* sex or race
and you don't have the *right* pedigree.

Imagine being well-aware that people are befriending you
because they need or want something from you.
Imagine taking them into your fold anyway
because you are taught to show up for others.

Imagine everything that you are "supposed" to be,
is inorganic to your nature –
you go along with it because being yourself is "crazy."
Then, if you can, imagine there being this forever-burning spark
inside of you that refuses to be suffocated by everyone else's
expectations.
That is resilience, that is confidence.
Confidence is understanding exactly who you are,
what you have or don't have and feeling secure.
Confidence is knowing you deserve
whatever brings you, the real you, unbridled joy.

## Self-Affirming

I am healthy.
I am pain-free.
I am wealthy.
I am safe.
I am a successful author.
I am an entrepreneur.
I am free.
I am confident.
I am beautiful.
I am kind.
I am peace.
I am strong.
I am honest.
I am wise.
I am intelligent.
I am clean.
I am generous.
I am trustworthy.
I am discerning.
I am patient.
I am wonderful.
I am prosperous.
I am whole.
I am decisive.
I am loving.
I am loved.

## Abiding Lies

You knew that I wanted to be loved,
and you used that desire to solicit strokes for your ego.
You allowed me to believe you were decent.
It wasn't until I started to descend
that I uncovered your lies.

## Power in Awkwardness

Knowing the odds does not make me any less confident
in our ability to upset the status quo.
In areas where barriers are set daily to slow our stride,
we rise, and we thrive.
We take the dirt thrown on our backs
and pave roads, blaze trails,
weather storms, and keep on going.
We are limitless, and it shows
in our come ups and comebacks.
We've learned to embrace our truths,
even when they are not popular,
because it's the only way to be free.
What we might deem as awkwardness in our personality
is really the power of our creativity

## Open Intimacy

I want to be in that intimate space with you,
where you're all about me and I'm all about you,
where, in every way, we connect like lovers do,
where we solidify our forever, and it's comfortable,
where love is present despite
what we're going through.
I want to be that way with you and only you,
the promise of forever is not just words;
it's what we're going to do.

# Holding Space for the Mundane

Please, tell me your story again,
the one that started in uncertainty.
I promise to sit, listen, and hold space for you.
Remind me of when everyone else saw mundanity,
while the intensity of what you couldn't grasp broke you.
We can keep a record of how many times you cried.
I want to know all about the shoulder you needed but didn't have.
Share the truth that speaks to your life's journey.
I'm in awe when you're clear about the turning points
and open enough to share how you learned about life.
I love your authenticity, you are so courageous.
I plan to burn the words into my memory
and hold the emotional weight in my heart.
Let me be a vault for your secrets.
Tell me all the things you couldn't say back when...

People wouldn't know it to look at you, but you still struggle.
Extend yourself some grace; healing is an ongoing process.
But I see your effort, and you get stronger every time you share.

Please, tell me your story.

## Traitor

Loud and clear, you said, "Be confident,"
then you tore her down.
She never had your time or attention;
if you mention her, it is not by name
but by the superficial dismissals of the vain.
She noticed that your head turned
for women who were everything she was not.
She spoke her truth to you,
but you called it a false narrative,
as if you did not see the pattern,
as if you did not contribute to it.
She bore the weight of your rejection
but did not reject you when you needed her.
When she needed you, you scolded her
to "be a strong Black woman."
When she spoke of her loneliness,
you reminded her she was "too independent."
She held on to your words,
patterned herself after your instruction
because you were the "leader."
You chastised and openly ostracized her,
and now this is where you are.
She has learned to survive without you;
she is proud that she is growing and flourishing.
She no longer believes you have her best interests at heart.
She sees your opportunistic acts for what they are
you are a vacuum of her strength.
She does not have a will to re-assimilate
to the covert hate she has faced.
Untamed love rises against ignorance,
causing old flames to die out.

Tempers flaring is welcomed
if the heat is fueled with passion
and the voices of pleasure are loud

## To My Tribe, With Love

I am Black, and I am a woman.
I am unapologetically both.
The complexity is that I am not more or less of either.
My compassion, my heart, my pride, my sorrow
all that I am, is drawn to those who share those qualities.
When I write, I'm drawn to address
those who hold my heart captive
and who cause my soul to stand at attention.
My ever-discerning eyes observe in awe
the change and growth happening
with those who belong to my tribe.
When they suffer, I suffer with them
sometimes openly, other times in lonely silence.
I cringe at their misconduct,
but I tough-love them through the process.
I applaud their efforts and cry tears of joy
at their success.
I carry their vision and support their dreams.
I am a part of them, even when I am apart from them.

## Seeking Wholeness

Dear God,
Show me what it is
Show me what's broken in me.
Show me where my life paused
and I became a walking shell.
Reveal to me the heart of the matter:
where are the shattered pieces of my being
that have been scattered.
Remind me of the past that
I can't remember.

Who am I?
Who am I supposed to be?
The old words, the previous antidotes,
are no match for the impenetrable walls around me.
And where did they come from?
With what did I build them?

Am I protecting me,
or those who are in danger
from getting too close?
For so long, I felt nothing
There was nothing.
But now, I feel the weight of everything,
all at once, unyielding.

## Queendom

We sat together...
I was offered chivalry and regimented affection.
I was offered a chance to be a chef,
housekeeper, nurturer,
sexual partner, and personal assistant.
He tried to spoon-feed me my being;
in exchange, I'd get to change my last name
and pretend to be satisfied.
I declined.
I offered him a seat at my table,
and he assumed he belonged at the head of it.
This sir, is a Queendom.

## Leave Me

Stop asking me to confine my being
to the smallness of your revelation.
My crown does not fall
just because I refuse to be controlled
by your limitations.
I was born to be guided
by the spirit within me;
I was not created
so you could tame me.
It's called freedom
it's called freedom indeed.
You urge us to be the best "us" we can be,
but what you mean
is to be what's best for you,
not what is best for me.

## Real Love

God is love.
An infinite flow of energy that is the source for all life
God is the personification of love
The presence of light in all we are and all we create
Whenever we lead with love, create with love, and receive in love
We are conduits of God.
What we offer in love is a gift from God.

## For the Love of the Diaspora

I watch the sneaky snakes we call skin folk,
parlay with the lepers for a foot in
or should I say, a foot on the backs
of the Blacks in this land.

The good ol' land of the free, for some.
They play deaf, blind, and dumb when they come,
as if they don't know of our ancestors' blood.
Our trauma is the reason they can breathe easily.
They believe they're so much more educated
because their savior said so,
yet they don't know the math:
Thinking the one percent will
provide them with half.

To them, it doesn't matter;
the propaganda has convinced them
that we are criminal and crazy.
They believe we lack culture and are lazy
it's laughable, but not funny.
It hurts that they sold out for a little bit of money.

But their time will come;
the viper always strikes
after you're comfortable.
But don't worry, we will advocate for you
we always do.

## The Illusion of Stability

Walking through life, checking off all the boxes,
doing all the things I'm supposed to do.
I venture off the path every now and then,
but I return, pulled back by fear—fucking fear.
Yet there's no need to regret it;
I've learned that I've already conquered
the fear of the unknown.
There is no such thing as safe.

## Unforgiving Shadows

You're not so different from the person you won't forgive,
from those to whom you don't extend grace
the ones who sit on the receiving end of your impatience.
You refuse to see the shadow that you cast,
how quickly you downplay your own impertinence.
The amplification of others' errors
while shying away from accountability
is an interesting choice.

# About the Author

Aimee Ebron is a writer and poet with a deep commitment to exploring human experience through words. With a background in Communication Arts and English Literature, her work often delves into themes of resilience, identity, and introspection. Aimee's journey is one of self-discovery, as she reflects on life's complexities and uncovers insights that resonate with readers from all walks of life. She brings a unique perspective to her poetry, combining personal growth with universal truths, and inviting readers to find strength in their own stories.

In her debut collection, *Beneath One Layer*, Aimee offers readers a contemplative exploration of life's hidden layers and the emotions that shape us.

**Connect with the Author:**
**Instagram:** @tobeaimee2
**Substack:** @tobeaimee
**Email:** aimeefreelance@yahoo.com

www.ingramcontent.com/pod-product-compliance
Lightning Source LLC
Chambersburg PA
CBHW020654060526
44119CB00069B/47